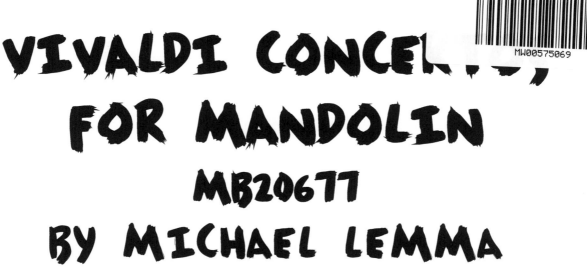

VIVALDI CONCERTOS, FOR MANDOLIN
MB20677
BY MICHAEL LEMMA

FREE GUITAR ACCOMPANIMENT PART AVAILABLE ONLINE!
VISIT: WWW.MELBAY.COM/MB20677

BILL'S MUSIC SHELF

Visit us on the Web at www.melbay.com or billsmusicshelf.com

Table of Contents

Program Notes

The purpose of creating these arrangements was to adapt three of Vivaldi's most beloved mandolin/lute concertos to a duo format. One of the challenges I enjoy about arranging music is creating a workable format that sounds complete in its new setting, while still retaining the original intent of the composer. I also believe in arranging accompaniment that sits comfortably under the fingers. Thus, the music becomes accessible to musicians at many levels. This arrangement is appropriate for performances from the living room to the concert hall. The solo part stays true to the original and can be performed by mandolin, guitar, violin or flute- almost any C instrument. The guitar part was arranged from the orchestra (string) parts and chord indications have been added to make the part flexible.

Concerto in A (RV82) was originally a trio sonata for lute, strings and continuo in the key of C major. By bringing it down to the key of A major, some of the higher ranges are kept within the first several positions. While many of the guitar parts are straightforward (block) chords, the guitarist should not be afraid to embellish the chords to complement the solo part, especially in the second movement.

Concerto in C (RV 425) was featured in the Oscar winning movie Kramer vs. Kramer, and is perhaps Vivaldi's best-known work for mandolin. Like many of the concertos of the Baroque period, soloists have the liberty to embellish or improvise on the melodic content in the second movement -- especially on the repeat. Sections without chords (marked "solo") should be played as written since it is a part usually performed by an orchestra musician such as a cellist. If you enjoy this work, listen to Vivaldi's Concerto in G for 2 Mandolins (RV 532)!

Concerto in D (RV93) may be one of Vivaldi's most popular works of all time and was originally for lute and strings (the modern guitar did not yet exist). Today, almost everyone performs the solo part on guitar. The arrangement will work particularly well for 2 guitars as well as mandolin and guitar. In the third movement, the soloist may choose to play the half notes as arpeggios or strum them with a vigorous 12/8 rhythm. Sections without chords (marked "solo") should be played as written since it is a part usually performed by an orchestra musician such as a cellist. Traditionalists should note that the opening motive was originally written:

The "RV" (Ryom Verzeichnis or Ryom index) indication is a cataloguing system by Peter Ryom, a Danish musicologist. It is one of a few systems used to catalogue and identify Vivaldi's compositions. There are many excellent recordings of these concertos and I encourage you to seek out and enjoy the interpretive differences in recordings of orchestras and various ensemble settings. I hope you have as much fun playing these works as I have had arranging and performing the music!

Concerto in A (RV 82)

Movement I

Arranged by Michael Lemma

Antonio Vivaldi

* Chords are for reference or embelishment.

Concerto in A (RV 82)

Movement II

Arranged by Michael Lemma

Antonio Vivaldi

* Chords are for reference or embellishment.

9

Concerto in A (RV 82)

Movement III

Arranged by Michael Lemma

Antonio Vivaldi

* Chords are for reference or embellishment.

11

This page has been left blank
to avoid awkward page turns.

Concerto in C (RV 425)

Movement I

Arranged by Michael Lemma

Antonio Vivaldi

*Chords are for reference or embellishment

Concerto in C (RV 425)

Movement II

Arranged by Michael Lemma

Antonio Vivaldi

Concerto in C (RV 425)
Movement III

Arranged by Michael Lemma

Antonio Vivaldi

*Chords are for reference or embellishment.

23

24

Concerto in D (RV 93)

Movement I

Arranged by Michael Lemma

Antonio Vivaldi

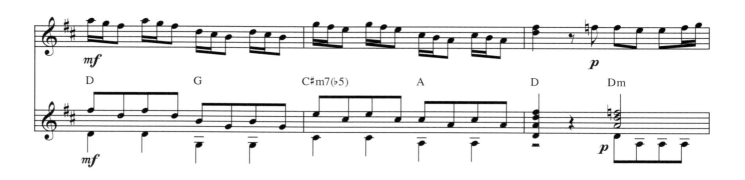

Note: The original manuscript has the opening motive as two 32 notes and a dotted eighth.
* Chords are for reference or embellishment.

27

29

Concerto in D (RV 93)

Movement II

Arranged by Michael Lemma

Antonio Vivaldi

* Chords are for reference or embellishment.

Concerto in D (RV 93)

Movement III

Arranged by Michael Lemma

Antonio Vivaldi

* Chords are for reference or embellishment.

** Chords may be strummed or arpeggiated.

Part Music

Mandolin

Concerto in A (RV 82)

Movement I

Mandolin

Arranged by Michael Lemma

Antonio Vivaldi

This page has been left blank
to avoid awkward page turns.

Concerto in A (RV 82)

Movement II

Mandolin

Arranged by Michael Lemma

Antonio Vivaldi

Concerto in A (RV 82)

Movement III

Mandolin

Arranged by Michael Lemma

Antonio Vivaldi

Concerto in C (RV 425)

Movement I

Mandolin

Arranged by Michael Lemma

Antonio Vivaldi

This page has been left blank
to avoid awkward page turns.

Concerto in C (RV 425)

Movement II

Mandolin

Arranged by Michael Lemma

Antonio Vivaldi

Concerto in C (RV 425)
Movement III

Mandolin

Arranged by Michael Lemma

Antonio Vivaldi

Concerto in D (RV 93)

Movement I

Mandolin

Arranged by Michael Lemma

Antonio Vivaldi

Note: The original manuscript has the opening motive as two 32 notes and a dotted eighth.

Concerto in D (RV 93)

Movement II

Mandolin

Arranged by Michael Lemma

Antonio Vivaldi

Concerto in D (RV 93)

Movement III

Mandolin

Arranged by Michael Lemma

Antonio Vivaldi

* Chords may be strummed or arpeggiated.

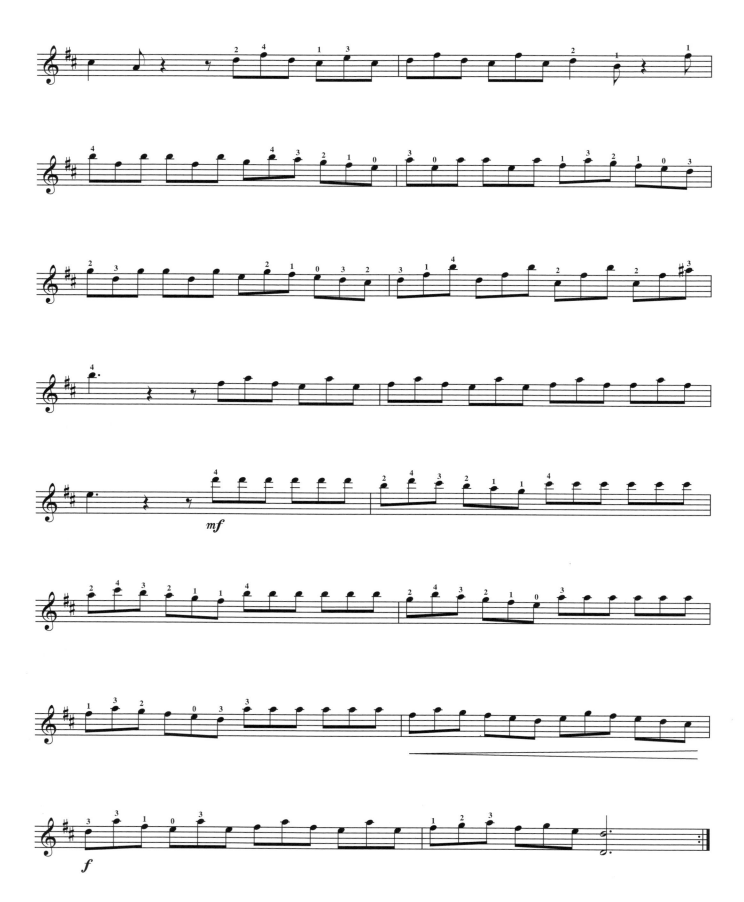

Michael Lemma

Michael Lemma counts himself fortunate to have a life in music- teaching, performing, listening, and helping others reach their goals. He is grateful for the gifts that music lends to humanity and truly believes it can affect the lives around us.

Michael has been Director of Music at a New Jersey magnet high school since 1994 where he established the nationally recognized program. He earned a Master of Arts degree in music from Columbia University and a Bachelor of Music degree in music education from Keene State College. He continues to perform in numerous venues from weddings to festivals. Highlights include Vivaldi's *Mandolin Concerto in C* with the North Jersey Philharmonic and Crumb's *Ancient Voices of Children*. Michael also presents educational clinics promoting the value of plucked string music in school music programs. His workshops have been enthusiastically received at organizations such as American String Teachers Association, Classical Mandolin Society of America, and MENC The National Association of Music Education. He was a member of New York Mandolin Orchestra, Bloomfield Mandolin Orchestra, and Director of National Guitar Workshop campuses throughout the United States. Michael is the founder and director of New Jersey Guitar & Mandolin Society.

Michael's students have been accepted to all levels of local and national honors ensembles, and study music at the nation's top universities. He has adjudicated for All-State Band/Orchestra festivals since 1994 and was Educational Adviser to the North Jersey Philharmonic, where he collaborated on projects that foster appreciation for classical music. He has received grants from Plucked String Foundation, Classical Mandolin Society of America, and NJ State Council of the Arts. Michael credits his many associations with musicians, teachers, students, songwriters, friends and family who have taught him much throughout the years.

UNIQUELY INTERESTING MUSIC!

7759112R0

Made in the USA
Charleston, SC
07 April 2011